Poetic Prose, Rants, &

Songs

(*Amidst a Pandemic*)

By Cole Holliday

Revolutionary Realism

We aren't communist
Capitalist
Republican or democrat
Liberal or conservative
Consumer
Animal

We are
American
Human
All made in God's image
Living is a God-given privilege
No matter any ideological difference…

Have you seen the news?
Or have you been burdened by distractions and your
personal blues?

Riots
Wildfires
Locusts
Lockdowns
Exodus to get out of town
Trump & Biden are 2 sides of the same coin
Hear the call to end the violence
The silence is deafening

Bad ideas sometimes materialize and cause the loss of life

Think through your opinions and mind your mind
Mind your mouth
Question your views and influences
Where's the truth in the midst of all these differences?

It's time to listen
And end the division

It's time to pray for the nation and the future of our
civilization to workout

It's time to mourn the lost men and women
And praise God for the babies being born
Hope comes with every next generation
We count on infants to end the wars in the middle east
Hey you toddlers, make a stand against climate change,
poverty, disease, disenfranchisement of lower classes, and so
on…
Get onto ousting crony-capitalists in government positions
And Cancel career and corrupt politicians
Then, silence the social-media-manipulation-masters

It's time for charity, unity, and a new vision of democracy
Not plagued by Big-Business interests

The people are the NATION

Something has got to give before the middlemen become
militiamen
Before the women and children become victims in the fight
for the right side of history
Before righteousness is redefined and repurposed

There's no sense in checking for a pulse, when *"Dead" is*
subjective – deliberate amongst yourselves until you smell the
rot
Then, question the reliability of your senses

We'll either live together or die together, but the common
man will not be remembered as the oppressor

March Covid Blues

I can't buy a mask

I can't wipe my ass

I can't eat a steak

I can't grab a drink

I'm forced to wait

I'm locked in my home and working to keep the lights on

I should be thankful to have a job

That's what the govt, family, and media tell me

They also tell me to stop living like I did a month ago

Flatten the curve and learn to obey

Only celebrities, rich people, and politicians get to live like

the world hasn't changed

<u>Tough Love for You</u>

You can't see the light
When you dwell in the dark
Dying is easy
Living is hard

Living through hell
You sold your soul online
You're waiting on heaven
All the time

Eyes fixed on matter
Matter melts the mind
Never counting all those sad hours
You spent scrolling through the night

You gave up on destiny
The past isn't far behind
Until you want to see
You'll always be blind

You chase your drinks instead of your dreams
You feed on distractions to quell your suffering
Until you start caring and you can dream,
You'll waste away in maddening misery

Tough Love for You 2

Narcissism and nihilism make up my feed in 2020

Survival of the fittest

"You do you, boo"

"Nah dawg, it's about me"

The vanity of you

The envy of me

(Amid a pandemic)

There is a growing need for charity

Love from above

To help those on the street

Now is a time like never to help out

Strength in numbers rather than selfish praise

I'm stuck in a country of prideful people who only pursue

pleasure

Married to the Highway

These lonesome highways haven't led me anywhere
I'm searching for something or someone somewhere

Maybe there's life under the neon lights
I only see the devil in sleepless nights

Loveless and lonely, I ramble these roads
I'll keep on going till I'm not alone

I sold my soul for a half-pack of cigarettes
I'm sad to say that I have bigger regrets

Like placing bets instead of buying a car
I should've learned the game before I played the cards

I sleep through the day just to die in the dark
I'll keep on sleeping till I see the stars

I can never get comfortable in any 1 place
I wait till the whisky is gone and the people start to
remember my name

It's time to move on
It's time to go away

I'm a shadow
A drifter

Always searching for a sign

I'm always 1 sigh away from hitching a ride
The highway will never escape my mind

Wide Eyed Girl 2

Wide eyed girl, you look so good to me

Close the book, and turn on the TV

Distract your mind with our reality

Look past the suffering of many

Open your mouth only to eat

Pay your bills, and chase your thrills

You'll be free

Red eyed girl, cling onto me

You shouldn't worry, because you're so pretty

You can spend your way to eternity, because there's no life outside of money

Fill up your cart and swipe that card

Learn to materialize the love in your heart

You can't save the souls that got lost at the start

You shouldn't show concern for people a world apart

Keep on spending
Do your part

Closed-eyed girl, look up to me

There's no truth, only consumption that leads to fiscal
certainty

Count the cost for civility

Question nothing and forget what you've seen

You'll be free

Miracle of You

I've been a drifter so long
Destitute and displaced
When I finally sought home
I was alone and afraid

I found the only one proven to ease my pain
The only one who could clear my name
And break these chains

I struggled while straddling the great divide
I pursued piety in pleasure
Only to kill the time

I believed a million lies
And buried the truth
You know I would have died
If not for you

The miracle of you is the life within me
A sinner gets saved
A saved man is free

Letter to the Lord

Lord, you saved me from my misery

I was battling devilish decisions and was sunk by my
consequences

Instead of realizing my destiny

You uncovered my eyes, and now I see

You laid down your life for sinners like me

You gave me life through your sacrifice

I live for the day

And sleep at night

You showed me my wicked ways

Now, I know what's right

I would have met the infinite grave

Through you

Oh, Lord

I am saved

A rant from November, an Election to Never Remember

It's time for the election
It's a final selection

It's going to be Biden or Trump
A dementia patient or a cancerous bump

Have your pick, America
Time's up

The donkeys and elephants are swimming in the same
swamp
(Hundred-dollar lily pads float across the murky waters near
Deficit Beach, and lobbyist frogs sit on rotting logs prepping
their speeches)

You better run
You best go hide
Buy a gun
Prepare to die…

I think I'll vote for democracy and turn off my phone
I don't know how I made it this far on my own

I see my tax dollars going overseas towards a 20-year-old
war
I see my brothers and sisters on the streets
Hitler and Stalin fanatics tell me I got to choose a side
"SiLeNcE iS vIoLeNcE" – Yeah right!

I'm unsure what's worth fighting for
It's hard to see the truth behind a mountain of lies

I don't have enough money for a President or even a third-party candidate
I buy from the companies that pay for the occupants in congress

There aren't any policies to bail out the poor
No matter about the hot mess that is hungry kids in every hometown across America

Only slugs and birdshot are left on the shelves
Only bad boys on the ballot

Plenty of advertisements begging for support

Woe to the bad boys in DC
Who are lining their pockets with you and me

We sell the world bullets and tell the citizens that more blood was spilled for our right to be free

An American Covid Overview for you

Landlords and repo men are making this year rough
If losing my job and making my home a prison wasn't
punishment enough…
I got the bank coming to auction my stuff

I cut up my credit cards
Changed my name
I had to sell my identity due to Covid-19

I haven't seen my family in 9 long months
All I see are drivers stopping at my neighbor's flat every
other day to drop off more stuff

The power company mails me often with threats to turn me
off
Question of ethics? … I think not

I'd give up everything for a bit of normalcy
However, it looks like my creditors are ahead of me

In America, I have the freedom to choose
You pay the winners on time, if you don't want to lose

I drive on an empty tank downhill to a food drive
As I wait in line, I get to see all my friends living their best
lives (in their homes on my phone)

If it weren't for my pride…

I'd ask for help from them to survive

Black Friday lost appeal after news of another suicide

When your stomach is growling, and you're burdened by
bills and internal despair
You have no appetite to buy online
Only left to scroll then stare

This consumer reality is in a steep decline
I'd go to church, if I could attend in real life

I wish I could hug a friend, see a full face,
Give a high-five, or a handshake

I'd compromise with just seeing the relevancy of time
Till then, and the government is making it clear that it's in
control of when, I'll just sleep between doorbell rings and calls
from collectors...

Maybe, just maybe, the world will start up again

Please somebody tell me that it's going to be fine
The fear of everyone dying has me counting every square
inch of where I reside

If I see another ad, I'll disable my neighbor's wifi

Cheers to the overlords, who are doing just fine

Once their servants go hungry, I guess society will unwind?

Oh, look at another football game, video, meme, joke, episode, and so many other possibilities through convenient streaming to waste my time

Stimulus Package

1,200 dollars so you won't burn down the city

1,200 dollars so you won't rape or murder anybody

1,200 dollars so you won't steal anything

1,200 dollars so you can say we did something

...

600 dollars?

How about 1,400 dollars?

Murder is at an all-time high

Stimulus Package 2

Oh, save your money
Better yet, shove it

I have no need for it
9 months of surviving the 99% apocalypse

Don't worry about my rent
I split 6 months ago

After the car ran down
I scrapped it for guns and ammo

You're a little late with the support

Politics played the people
Starved out the poor

My dreams are ashes
I can't even pray in the steeple

There are no red or blue constituents in the food lines
Only hungry people, who are sick of the times

Give us food
Tell the truth

Print us the palaces where the DC Kings reside

Doth thou congress count our votes or only collect our
tithes?

Companies come first, military next, and all the
downtrodden are cancer or terrorists

While the rich get richer
I'm getting thinner

It's going to be a dark dark winter

Feeble Minded

The reaction of people today is proof that they were distracted. Our bubbles popped and routines dissolved. The real plague is the reality of how fragile life can be. The illusion masked by entertainment and consumerism has become increasingly murky. The light is starting to pierce through. How to live, over what to do. So, pluck out at third eye, son. The smoky doors of perception that we all bought keys to, only led to subfloors with more doors to resentment and mostly coping mechanisms. You don't have to get lit to realize you are standing in shit. You've been bought and sold, tossed and turned, flipped and rolled, cooked then burned. Left as grease for the greater machine. Now, in sobriety and clear eyes you can see that you're a thinking and beautiful being with purpose and dreams. In turmoil and strife, you can't see any glimpse of destiny. God becomes greater than the occasional genie you seek in desperation. Christ died so that all shall live, but we've been too busy dying and buying, to truly consider him. Now that we're all woke and holed up in our shrinking homes, we have time to realize that we were never alone. Seek the truth and stop wasting your youth.

March Madness

I saw what I hope is the worst before the plague even hit
My neighbors in small town America became strangers in an
instant

Throwing their cash to enlarge their stashes of food, ammo and
toilet paper
Fear murdered manners…
Morality, kindness and compassion were violently thrown
out the window, once the wind of uncertainty blew in
Buyer's remorse will hopefully set in
I pray for clarity, civility, courage and charity
Hopefully, the elderly and disabled have all that they need
I saw a few humans post food offers to whoever in need
Thank God for those people!
Good grief, charity cases are multiplying by the dozen when
there's not one covid case within 70 miles of our city
Now, the not so humble or helping citizens sit on an
overindulgent mass, which they'd argue is between not enough
or getting by
Never plenty
I'm not mad
I'm just sad and confused
I envy the mountain man who got away because he lost his
faith in men
But not wholeheartedly because I wouldn't believe him
There's still a part of me that truly believes that this
revelations- preliminary-battle will bring out the best of people
We can't all get away, learn to chop wood and plant seeds

I can

However, what good is crop if there are no people to feed?

After the plunder, sleep well knowing we have yet to see hell

My city is charred already

The pale horse will be riding in on ashes

Any way, we'll have to wait

Make sure your guns are loaded for that thieving serial-rapist

who may ring your doorbell camera

Too many movies and too much news

Just in time for the indoor blues

Sober

Sobriety is the first step
Moving forward with a clear mind
with no time to look back
Visions are greater than today or tonight
The soul aged quick while stumbling through time
I arrived at the graveyard, but didn't want to die
Regrets pushed aside along with the whiskey and wine
Freed from bondage by the blood of Christ
One way to go
No longer leading myself blind
The demons I had to once quell in drunken hell
Were long gone when I saw the light
Good vibes no longer had to be poured over ice
The truth guides the will to get right
Take off those bourbon shades and see the sky
You don't have to die drunk to realize there's more to life

Don't be so Morbid

I've been down so long and stuck rationalizing my innate
ability to express morbidity
I've been called out on it many a time
Yet, I wouldn't call it an outlook on life
I always see the bright side
Even when my face is in dog shit
I have one eye peeking towards the sky
Buzzkill, maybe
Unwarranted and unholy expressions of my dark reflection
Have me reflecting on my inner-self, morality and drive to
keep living
Yeah, we are all going to die
Yeah, you got to be on God's good side
I confuse my depression with realism
I have regressed to half-witted statements of fatalism
Mortality is obvious
Salvation, not so much
Value of life, depends on who you ask
Finally, I end this unwarranted rant…
I want to steer away from morbidity entirely
As the subject of death has consumed me
Ruled me
Deceived me
Oh boy, through Christ we are free from all inequities
No shame or regrets
No longer a slave to the past, alive in the present
Death hath no power over you or me
We are free!

Sober 2

I keep whiskey in the fridge to remind me that I don't drink
Cigarettes in the freezer to keep me smoke free
Oh, how I sometimes long to dull this reality mixed with
misery with a sizeable portion of iced whiskey
Oh, how I sometimes wish to be drunk smoking till I can't
breathe
Oh, these temptations I've placed in my everyday sight
Have shown me that life is day and night
That you don't have to be fucked up all the time
Oh boy!
How bright life can be with sober eyes!
May these inanimate and suicidal tools no longer be considered
relief
Despite any adversity
How many sober weekends have you had?
Older people and peers always told me that sobriety comes
with maturing, whilst sipping their favorite poisons
Huxley impacted me by making a case that humans can't deal
with selfhood
In my practiced sobriety, I see that some people can't deal
with who've they come to be
Insecure people, people in pain, lost people, stressed
people, people who can't satisfy their needs, etc.
I trivialize the problems
Yet, I have a problem will people trivializing their potentials
Do you know how to be free from bad habits that give pleasure
only temporarily?

COVID RANT – "I KNOW MY RIGHTS"

Yeah, we shut down society and crushed small-business
dreams, but for the betterment of the machine
We know now that the people are submissive and weak
That they'll believe anything as long as they're not living on
the street
Hoax or no hoax, what does this power mean?
It means you are not free
Police will write you a citation if you are doing anything other
than shopping
I think of the gold rush travelers aware of Mormons and
Indians they'd face along the way
How they took the risk, however stupid, brave all the same
Stay inside for as long as you like
It's your forced duty, not your right
I saw kids attempting to swim at a nearby creek, cops wrote
them all up, and sent them home
What will they grow up to believe?
What's the point of civility or society when we are forced
home?
The last days may be fast ahead, but the illusion of
sovereignty is already dead
The nazis used willful-idiots (brown shirts) and propaganda
before the SS
If you don't think our capitalistic leaders won't do the same,
you best hold your breath
It's a nightmare of sorts that the working class can no longer
work

Dependent on Orwell's big brother for all his mischievous
support
Can't trust the media
Can't trust the government
Consumerism killed democracy and sold out the republic
Buy buy buy before you die, or the mighty US won't recover
Oh brother!
We are pawns in a game
We are born unique, but treated the same
It's hard to get uncomfortable when you're stuck in your home
It's hard to reach out when you and everyone else is prisoned
alone
I can't speculate on what's the come, the Bible says there's
nothing new under the SUN
If this is tribulations, then we haven't even begun
No suggestions to make use of your time, only a big rant
swirl around in your mind
I wish I had the answers, no doubt, during this terrible
passing of time
Perspective changes frequently and that's no lie
Wisdom without truth turns out to be an old living lie
Wake up to be the tide
What's life like when you're confined?

Gratitude of a Lucky Man

Life is beautiful and so are you

How bored you must be with nothing to prove

Impatiently waiting for some good news

Comfort and groove

Pending, what the world has left to go through

Weeks or months left of uncertainty

Certainly, the world won't be the same as it was in January

You're so pretty with your new attitude

Outlook grander from this point view

Life is precious and painful

Curious and cruel

Wonderfully enduring, but for a limited time

Scrapping that 5 year plan by asking the big questions in life

That 9 to 5 was an illusion exclaiming that the grind is the only way to survive

That glittered career path is now carved out of your mind

Oh baby, I love those blue-green-eyes

Those same eyes that are opened wide

Seeing the fragility of everything that you once thought was fine

How you maintain positivity in times like these is a mystery to me

Positively, you were always the star of my life, but I am in awe of your shine

Good or bad, however this turns out, I'm excited and thankful that you're mine

It's Not About me, It's About the Poetry

It's not about me
It's about the poetry
It's about explaining things as they seem
About distinguishing reality from the dream
My soul is a drifter stuck in a stationary body
Suffering in solace awaiting an escape that is destiny
When the soul meets the body in the grand awakening
The inner roots shoot out from the eyes and mouth with
memories of every sight and sound
What was simple becomes profound
To see the bigger meaning
The earth isn't floating on some uncharted course, there is
order in the universe

Death of George Floyd and Aftermath

All photos and videos on social media and television should be shown in black and white to symbolize wrong and right. The killer cop has been jailed justly. However, the acts of people across various cities around the nation paint a very ugly picture for America. Frankly, I am disgusted after viewing the million tiktok videos this week. Celebrities and activists invoking MLK quotes to rally the riots and destruction of businesses and consequently livelihoods, makes me think of how the nazis quoted the Bible to quell the Churches' concerns. Y'all got MLK mixed up with some extremists and history won't be kind writing this chapter. How dare anyone use the Black Lives Matter hashtag to show solidarity with that movement. How dare Black Lives Matter passively witness the destruction. This is an uprising to society and order. I've realized why America didn't make it into the book of Revelations. Our economy is doomed and society with it, if this country doesn't get with it and repent. If we commit evil acts, then God will leave us to our own consequences. America has yet to see much wrath.

George Floyd, an African American, was murdered. It took too long to arrest his killer... Sadly, the riots continue. This isn't about him at this point. This is about being broke, being woke, being nihilistic, being rebellious, being ungrateful, and being disrespectful to everything our ancestors and families built for us. It's time to talk about police brutality and racism. It's time to talk about the black men that fill up the prisons and graves from police action.

It's also time to talk about evil, raising children, keeping the family together, getting back to church, doing good in the community, serving the Lord, and finally being accountable for our own actions. God made us in his image, his fingerprints are all over the universe, from the millions of galaxies to your DNA. We need to acknowledge this and return to him. United we stand, or united we dissolve into our own hell.

Any Direction Would be Good About Now

The world is on fire

Your point of view is skewed

Conflicted in the times

Tormented by the news

Videos plague your mind

You're convinced we're doomed

Close your eyes

You're so tired in your search for truth

Quick Write

Pain and rage stuck in our face

In these last days

Real justice and peace are only a few pages away

People of this small world are confused and afraid

Uncomfortable in new strange ways

Every day is a blessing

Every choice for loss or gain

The loss could mean everything

To shine or to fade

Be better or waste

Dreams seem distant when you're forced into a daze

I'm Asking for 1 Good Day

I just want one good day from beginning to end

A day when:
My dogs listen to my first call
My work notices me
Only good news
My thoughts aren't trivialized

Enough about me

A day when:
No kid goes hungry
There's a cloudless sky
Where there's no disease
Where no one dies or cries
Everyone appreciates life

I had a good day until I read about a local man who killed
himself on a bridge in my hometown
He was 31 and made permanent choice... "Suicide rates are on
the rise"
Experts everywhere convincing kids that there's no meaning in
life, and the experts aren't surprised. People are the problem
and the cancer of this existence to every proclaimed scientist /
nihilist. Organic matter derived from lucky star dust turned out
walking around forgetting the importance of their dream with

low self-esteem. Good thing nothing has a meaning.
I'm cynical and sarcastic in this moment, but not yet bitter.
When you become bitter it's because the world made you
submit and quit. Oh, no one cares if you're indifferent, but
soon they'll care to know that your cares align and conform.
What about the cause?
You aren't blameless or shameless, are you?
Check on your friends, you bone bags and hypocrites. Check
on your family too!
Call your mom, you never call...
Get right with God before your ticket is punched.
Don't give up!
Every day you get is a blessing, make sure your time is well
spent.
You and future you, deserve it.

A Cause is Lost in the Content

It's not about the cause
It's about the content
Whatever can provoke the ever-growing mindful minds
To share, give reactions and make moves in real life
The video clips and big headlines
To make rushed conclusions
You're no martyr
Just a soldier on the Devil's frontlines
Deployed to kill the times and time
Reshape the future!
Go big or stay blind (Bullshit)
What once was thought to be sensational, overarching,
embellished, became full blown propaganda leading hundreds
of millions to publish manifestos online
Secret societies now prancing in the street, saying come on son,
destroy your city and fulfill your meaning!
We were handed keys to a digital world with a promise of
world peace
We were led to the desert as leaderless sheep, searching
endlessly for the Sea of Salvation
What a world!
Which turned out to be another tool by the world elite to
bend and control our reality
Like for part 3, subscribe to my link, you don't have to care
what i say...
I don't care about you or what you think.

I just want your money

Long live the powers that be

Some of whom openly want to enslave me

Cheers to your distractions!

May you live long enough to realize you cheated your destiny.

(W/ a long stare at the sky, reflecting every memory that meant something that you passed by, regrettably...)

Throw some gravel in the growing divide or build a bridge

It's a matter of a few power moves before you're locked into a permanent distraction

It your future, kids

Live free or die in sin

Not just where were you when it all happened... but who are you now, and who were you then...

Changeling, yeah right

Good luck in changing

Find a friend in discipline

Find disciplined and moral friends

Self-control and servitude can change your point of view

Seek truth

What Version of you is the truth?

The devil is on your heels all the way to the grave
That's okay as long as you don't stay too long in 1 place
Reminiscent of Dylan's never-ending tour, if it wasn't before,
it is now
Anyhow, it's strange how we grow, and how experiences
and faith take hold of us It's crazy how there are a million new
ways to grow up
Do you recognize who spits back at you in the mirror?
Is the past far behind and is the future near?
2 questions there, take your time
Tom petty says it's time to get going

C.M. – "Make a move, you may live once, but you will die twice if you never try". □□□ Don't wait on age for some revelation. The future is the present and past compact and moving fast for the complacent.

Lots of Talk of Revolution

You want a revolution

You can't fill the gap

You want the freedom of lawlessness

Until outlaws run the pack

Where order fails

Disorder reigns

There are many different runners in this revolutionary race

They all want to rule the place

The devil leads his disillusioned dogs into the fiery lake

We've politicized civil rights

We've made judgement on rights to life

We've celebrated evil

We've cursed our creator

We've went all-in on revolution with nothing to wager

We've forced beliefs on our neighbors

We've hung the individual

Doxed and threatened him

We've redefined right and wrong

To cover our sin

We've become emotion-led hypocrites left to live in a muddy

puddle, but calling it a cause

America, the melting pot, has become Americans in a box

A box with trip wire to control thoughts (America, the time-

bomb packaged in an Amazon box)

We broke all the mirrors, so no chance at reflection

We've created virtual gallows with prepared ropes to hang our

necks in

We can't always think in absolutes

When you believe a lie, you don't seek the truth

You can't post bail on a life sentence
Freedom from sin can only come from repentance

Old Mind

My body is young, but my brain has aged

Though my memories fade, the trauma remains

I reflect honestly and look at my past entirely

I remember things as they should have been, looking back
again

I see the butterfly effect

Oh, How the word "no" would have worked out better than
"yes"

Rewards and disasters merely noted as consequences

Simple phrases strike repeatedly in bold letters across my
mind like headlines running across the bottom of every news
outlet

I am sincere in my lament, watching the recordings in my
mind of how time came, and time went

Lest I forget

Damned, if I forget

The pain isn't the same as yesterday, every morning delivers
a fresh take

Yet, I ponder purpose and destiny, those questions became
quests in pursuit of certainty

Certainly, death isn't as bothersome as the next cruel
memory

Misery lingers as the vulture, and every time I suffer, I
suffer in multitudes as the beak rips the flesh

I digress...

Again, I see things through honest lenses

Looking back, I was blind in all my senses

I didn't believe in gravity

I couldn't feel the weight of my burdens, even though the
mass was crushing me
I still have my ticket stubs from the times I bought into the
charade
My eyes are fixed
God help me, so that I never look away

Letter to Baby

She shoots gummy bear shots and curses alot

She hasn't cursed me yet

The wildness she exhales in every breath, wears me out

I may be old and mean

Yet, her optimism prevails

Counter attacking every morbid feeling that slips from my
mumbling mouth

She embodies a sense of innocence

My dear lady, the world will break you yet

I don't even dream of anything so foul

She's the joy of my being

She erases my suffering

With a smile so overwhelming it flips a frown and curves these
slanted eye brows

The suffering filled lines in my big forehead often fade in her
presence, and run flush with my blushed face

Misery dissipates when she looks my way

She takes insecurities and crushes them into a million pieces

She's pretty funny too

She sees past my grievances and conveniently skips over my
cynicism

She calls out the bullshit as a lover, as an empathetic critic

Never condemned, but honest and true

She's one a million with a rare yet profound point of view

Dear lover, I don't what I'd do without you

Lockdown Rant

These months without sports or celebrities really give
chance for remedy
At least reflection to think through the deception
We're insane and morally depraved
We'd rather be entertained than be brave
Brave to face reality, our problems, the world's problems, etc...
The hard truth is that our time is paid towards distractions
We're sucked in and blind to see what's really happening
The money spent on football and movies could feed all of
humanity, home the homeless, and fund fixes to slow climate
change
The system that we cover our hearts for and salute was only
built to protect you
The giant killing machine isn't the root of society
The people the system swear to protect are the nation
A government led by people should be for the people
People are what makes America free
I digress… Back to idolatry…
Where you spend your dollars today will define what will
remain after this plague
There will be more homeless, more hungry people (children, if
that'll get your attention), more closed businesses (sorry ma &
pop), more suffering (Africa is in the midst of a plague and
famine that the world has never seen)
Your money is defines your motives and your mind
Mind your money, then spend with your heart for the sake
humanity
Quit spending just to pass the time

Oceanview Blues

The giant waves of a tropical storm crash into the shoreline
in thunderous calamity
The lightning in the distance where the sky meets the sea
Thunder rumbles and echoes like a bullhorn in a mile-long
cave
Penetrating winds blast sand and water bullets into the backs of
beach goers
(Who are enduring the torture for the spectacle)
The spectacle of nature in her fierce wrath as she churns the
waters rapidly and sends her ocean army to storm the beach
The sky is painted by God with shades of green and pink, a
beautiful warning of what's to come
With bullish thunderheads stampeding towards the mainland
The equalizer in humanity are the natural disasters
We can appreciate and respect weather as it's indiscriminate
and unbiased
A product of sin set to crash or spin in its charted or uncharted
course with no bias and no remorse
Weather doesn't consider victims or hear the pleas
If you sit though the storm and survive, then you can see how
small you are with all your plans and dreams

Oceanview Blues 2

I stare into the vastness and belittle my dreams
Life in the city seems so important until you're facing the sea
Those responsibilities, relationships, bills, calls, emails, dms,
and texts
All sounding endlessly while trying to find a place to settle
down in certainty
Infinitely searching for meaning and debating what's worth
achieving
Get to the beach and the matters melt instantly
It's a matter of changing the mind's frequency by
comparing my small thought box to the size of the sea

Writer's Block All Summer Long

I waited the whole summer to write the words I wanted to say...
The words never came

I tuned my guitar to turn my moods into melodies...
I didn't want to play

I bought colors, brushes and canvases...
I didn't have anything to paint

I tried self-cures through exercise, diet, and vitamins...
I still feel the same

I went on adventures...
I never really escaped

I wanted to ask God for help...
I never prayed

My mind is imprisoned in a body that is imprisoned in a home,
and home is supposed to be safe...
I tell myself and everyone else that everything is okay

Normalcy was buried alone in an unmarked grave...
The world and social media tell me that times are finitely
strange

What a world to return to...
Well for me, I'll be Forever changed

COVID RANT 2

I saw the biggest and most beautiful sky this morning on my 2,100th commute

During this drive, I try to decide what could unite the country. War came first to mind... A common external enemy to fight for the sake of our liberty. Unfortunately, I arrived at work before I could consider all the options... A lot of the population seem convinced that a civil war is imminent. Clashes of ideologies with blood spilled on city streets, the barbarians are always at the gates. Choose a side, prepare to die. Really depressing shit... Woke folks shooting holes through Covid lies, while telling me I got to buy a gun to sleep at night. Cities razed, people still unemployed, protests continue, riots continue, anger and violence on the right and left sides. Most people are divided by who they vote for, where they shop, who they're friends are, etc. Lots of sheep and only bad shepherds.

Lots of generalizations… At any rate, Libtards and Nazis playing battle royal on the city streets for their claims of what exactly? Movements monetized to make politics materialize, and tell me what difference any current movement is making on either side? Where's the money to help the poor and hungry. Eventually, if we don't unite, most of us will all be hungry, radicalized, and ready to fight to survive. The rest will be victims of times.

Chin up, Chest Out, Mouth Closed, Eyes Fixed, to be Star bound

Life moves fast when you're living in the past
I'm sure that's been said through the millennium
Patch up that third eye and get out the shit
Life is complicated when you're tossed into the mix
Present problems supersede the past
Your future is uncertain, so make a mark that will last
You're someone, not just anyone, with a talent specially
assigned to you
Your wits and talents are tools for your destiny
Don't let time slip away, don't live in complicit animosity
As long you're working and as long as you still dream,
everything you seek can be seen
Straighten yourself out and fix your eyes, you are the victor
or the cause of your own demise
Doubt is a cancer that can easily spread, dying is the same
as dwelling on regrets
Don't leave your potential untapped, you simply do not
have time for that
Life is precious and sacred; you are a piece of art in the
making
When you're beneath the neon lights, you can't see he stars
in the sky
When you're trapped in your head cycling through
decisions and memories, you may miss a true moment meant to
endow you into scenic serenity

Look what surrounds you, then recognize the enormity of life
outside of how you plan to spend your time
God paints masterpieces on the regular, and all you have to
do is look up
The sights are liberating
The beauty of it all are the brief moments in awe which
trivialize was the discontent I feel in the daily grind
The world is on fire literally and figuratively, and there's
nothing I can do about it in the big scheme of THE WORLD...
The world will keep spinning on its plotted and orderly course,
and we will all be here questioning our self-worth
No matter what movement, this planet will keep moving,
maybe even after kingdom come
Love with all you got, fight for all you have, remember all
you've had, and see the good despite the bad

There's a plan for you, and we've all got something to prove
What do you have to lose?

Love of a Rambling Man

I've been east and west, Miami to Los Angeles

I've made several stops in the Rockies and never thought of
who I was abandoning

"Go where the gold is" is what I was told often as a kid

I didn't find any gold in Austin, Dallas, or Houston

Miami, Orlando, or Pensacola

Colorado Springs, Denver, or Salida

Los Angeles, San Diego, or Anaheim

Vegas, Bullhead city, or anywhere in the □ desert

OKC, Tulsa, or Muskogee

St. Louis, Wichita, or Kansas City

New Orleans, Lafayette, or Shreveport

Memphis, Vicksburg, or Mobile

I did like Murfreesboro, AR though, but not enough to leave
my family at home Every city a wonder of its own, lacked the
love I've only ever known

The lure of starting anew, is the gypsy curse that lives in
my roots

The curse is a myth, and love is the truth

I bought a home only 10 minutes from my parents, and I
can't wait till the next trip

Next time around I'm not looking for gold on foreign ground

My gold was at home all along, family is a goldmine most
profound

Triggered by Twitter, Facebook, & Youtube

All the ammo is gone, the nation is polarized, the media
sells us fear, social media sells us, and it's time to get back to
living life
Social media, the masters of systematic slavery
Left victims penniless and angry
Convincing them endlessly to spend their way out of misery
When the work stopped and the ads continued
The slaves grew maddened, confused and blue
All that buying never taught them about crisis or what to do
The situation grew grave when the slaves realized they could
buy time to get through or escape
For weeks, the oxygen of information left their saturated brains
and the dopamine was drained

Then one day (some day), they started to blink
Then breath
The aches and tremors of addiction faded away
They no longer weep when their chains can't fulfill their needs
The need for relevance and the feeling of satisfaction that
comes from purchasing material things and constant
affirmation, dissipated back into the virtual abyss
The abyss that is void of whole truth, fulfillment, and
meaning
They looked out the window and realized they were locked
inside
The buildings and cars on fire, cities conquered by rioters of
the different Reich's Surrounded by blue lights
Nothing left to do, nothing left to buy

Watching out the window and trying not to cry
They deactivated their chains, left their homes, then joined the
fight
Now, the social media masters don't go out at night

COVID RANT 3

You're all worth it. If the election taught us anything, it's a nation divided. Our government sucks at everything, and only works in the interests of corporations and banks. Red or blue, they don't care about you. Biden bailed out the same guys that Trump plays golf with. The conservative and liberals took on new definitions in the last 4-5 years, hell, the whole dictionary will be rewritten in the next 5 to 10. As the world battles Covid and famine, and conveniently ramps up for a war… If you're still living, you got to find something or someone worth living for. Keep fighting. Keep giving. Keep praying. Keep loving. The future maybe dismal, but the sting won't be worse than you not tapping into your full potential. Your dreams and goals are waiting to be realized. Time isn't on your side, time is a temporary allowance to make a memory and find a family. Life is precious and sacred; life is more valuable than all the profits Amazon and Walmart made during the pandemic. Far more substantive than any material possession.

Fake Friend

Swindle little snake
Make a sucker out of me again
I have nothing to lose
You were my only friend
I guess she's just a girl
And you're a devil of a man
You were once strangers in my world
Now, we're enemies until the very end
You can stop calling now
Your apologies make me sick
Just 1 night ruined our relationship
You did something so bad
But you sure had fun
The past is hurtful
What's done is done
She's a slut and you're a bastard
So long to the good times
Nothing ever good, ever lasted
I guess she was my girl and you're the devil
I divided my eggs into 2 baskets
Now, I'm empty handed and saddened

Bye Bye Baby

My baby doesn't love me like she used to
She doesn't hug me when I'm blue
I look at her and she turns the other way
I ask her what's on her mind
She doesn't have much to say
My baby, my baby has gone far away
She never says what's wrong
And nothing is ever more than okay
I get so lost in her growing suffering
Lord, help see what she wants me to see
If I didn't hear her stomping the floor or slamming the doors
I wouldn't know what we were fighting for
Even when she's here, she's never home
I think it's clear, she wants to be alone
At least she's feeling something
Probably something awful
Her happiness dissolved when I couldn't give her the whole world
I'd get her flowers if she thought I was thoughtful
My baby, my baby is in a depraved state
All I can do is guess the other man's name
I wish she would open up and be frank
Maybe Frank is his name
Anyway, I'm bleeding inside pleading her to ease the pain
I wish I could read her mind
Then free our lives
I'm stuck in a hell of a time
Trying to keep this love alive

When she screams in my face
I can only play the same game
I'd say she is crazy if I hadn't already
gone insane
Oh, depressed lover, look up from your phone
I can't imagine a life on my own
You mean everything to me
Oh baby, please don't leave…
My baby, my baby left without a letter or saying goodbye
I'm sure she's out there with some other guy
In silent suffering, now alone in this cruel world, I stare
painfilled and patiently out the window

Hey Layla

Hey Layla, Hey Layla

Don't look at me like that

You are the best, the very best friend that I will ever have

Hey Layla, Hey Layla

It didn't mean anything

I was drunk, lonely, lost in a moment, and I didn't want
your heart to break

Hey Layla, Hey Layla

Please unpack your things

I'll give you the whole wide world because you're my girl

I even bought you a diamond ring

Hey Layla, Hey Layla

Please don't drive away

I deleted her number

I got sober

I'm hopeful you'll see and appreciate my change

Hey Layla, Hey Layla

Unblock me from your phone

It's been a whole long month, and I can no longer be alone

Hey Layla

Hey Layla

Hey

Layla

Please come home

Prayer to The New-Age Deity

Dear extraterrestrial being,
Only so high
May you guide us through our evolving perceptions of life
and value of lives
If your deity is true, please show passivity as we change
definitions, rewrite history, and determine our own destiny
May our emotions always be greater than or equal to truth
You must always acknowledge and accept our truths
May the future always be in the hands of the youth
May we bend our enemies until they convert or break
May we ruin their livelihoods and make them desperate for
our way
May we never forgive the offenders, and forget their
existence (even if they change)
Tolerance through dominance
Through final justice, we will know true peace and grace
We will force-feed our ideas, which will be consumed and
shared by all human race
Woe to the ignorant and distracted, as they'll be our slaves
We aim to make it obvious, everyone will know their place,
and won't succumb to the capitalistic illusions of past decades
May the radicals of today, be the martyrs of tomorrow
Oh, good being, see our great plans
Let the dwellers of this corrupt planet understand
Curse our dissenters and let them be slain
The revolutionary heroes are to be celebrated throughout
history and to be eternally praised (if not worshipped)

Let the revolutionaries reveal themselves as the true global
chain
The heads of the absolute solution
Until we discover the missing link, we pray in your gender-
neutral name

Amen, Awomen

Most Intriguing Old Chap

"Most intriguing, old chap"
I thought for no apparent reason while standing naked in the
kitchen
Now... Questioning the extent of damage that my brain has
taken
Years of alcohol abuse and addiction
Still in sufferable denial while faced with constant affliction
Maybe there was a chance to have changed the outcome,
maybe I was born as no one
Rum-a-dumb-dumb-Opiods-in-the-tub-and-thoughts-in-the-
blender-landlord-left-town-and-abandoned-the-renters
Maybe a sobering thought may come again
Bringing kind memories devoid of cruel reflection
Then, I'll forget it happened
Woe to the fool on the couch that's blacked out
He'll be dead soon and never missed, tis a shame
They die all the same
I'm left to be a clever, but bitter fool
Never to age, but remain a ghost of a beautiful loser (to very
few)
In memoriam, what's new? (Progress, Future, Foresight,
Optimism, Optimus Prime, Amazon Prime)
Bitten by the snake of lies
Poisoned inside
Stuck in moods of uncertainty and indifference
Never learning or appreciating any divine or circumstantial
consequence

Radically mutated perception left dying under a black light
Dismal reality surfing while seeking (and never seeing) the
sunlight
Stress made strife
Surely everything after this will be all right
The enlightening drugs made me blind!
Leading this sucker of a soul left to drift through a dense fog
of torture in dwindling time

"Love Wins" Says The Bitter Old Fool

I'm at the end of my rope
I can't stand to read the news
Much less hear a joke
The depravity has spread like lymphoma
And I'm a white-blood cell cowering in a plaque-filled
artery
God help me
I hate the word bitter, but I've grown to hate the world
The radicals on the left and right (both of which are telling
me I must pick a side) (silence is violence, yeah right)
Too many causes and people have died in the fights
Blood flows in the streets, and only smashed buildings are
relics of the times
The lawmakers
The expanding laws and restrictions
The forfeit of privacy
The sexualizing of children
The devaluing of humans
The destruction of family
The nihilism of many
The lack of charity
Lack of companionship and community
The ad campaigns
Political campaigns
The wars overseas
Uncle Sam deciding what's best for me
Social media selling my browsing and buying history

The govt spying and killing endlessly to keep us free
McCarthyism galore
And frankly, I'm sore
I'm sick
But it's not because of Covid, and I had that 2 months ago
Funny enough, I'm still stuck at home
My fellow humans are arguing about genders on their
phones
Most without the slightest recognition of the enormity of
life
I don't want these poor bastards to conform to my views or
see with my eyes
I simply want them to look up to the sky
I'm no saint to pass judgement, but judges are stomping out
the saints
Provoking the worst of humanity
In a time when the best of humanity is needed
My goodness, we need goodness

LOL

Another ad

Another meme

Another distraction

Dusty dreams buried in jokes

Ambition melted down into false hope

Trading time for videos and liking posts

Too many reflections and not enough time

Missing opportunities while trying to unwind

Time moves forward

The humans grow old

Don't forget to save, so you can buy

Don't worry about living, until it's time to die

Oh, by the way, you'll never know when

So, don't worry till then

Live for now

Swipe, swipe, swipe

Like, like, like

Faded into Dreamland

Hit your Zen Pen
Then, take a nap
Your routine is a coping mechanism
A mechanizing trap
The bliss of blinded perception leads the blind man into
disillusionment and foggy reflection
Potential is put on hold by blocking that stranger of a soul
The heart is wicked, and the mind lies
You never listen to either
You only fade through time

A Critique You May Disagree With

We're a generation of full-grown kids who take commercial
supplements
We have long hair and thin skin
We can self-deprecate in a moment's notice, and we drink
heavily between vape hits
We breathe revolution yet have profiles on LinkedIn
We live vicariously through influencers, and even fund them
We have hundreds of causes and millions of posts
All looking for affirmation from people who we admire the
most
Cause or content, content for the cause
We've let our dreams dissolve
We've sown disillusionment and reaped videos and memes
We're between enlightenment and lost
We've defined irony and we violently impose pity
We are never thankful, and resources will never be plenty
Our boredom manifested into blogging our daily lives, and
we gave away our privacy to elite villains (who we vocally
despise)
We are hypocrites and only focus on self-love
We will destroy the lives of anyone who doesn't think like
us
We see the world through tinted shades and are reminded
that money is the root of change
While the ice caps melt away, and the ozone dissipates, we
continue posting our days away

Our generation is neither truthful or brave, we speak words,
but don't believe what we say
We are hypnotized by phones and scrambled by
information
We are the true last mindful, but spineless, generation

Nihilists and violence to come
We will look at the ashes and ask, "What have we done?"
[A revolution fixed on the exploitation of suffering and pain
will only produce victims in the trials of change]

Plague of Reflection, you Look too Deep

Why the long face and the hollow eyes?
Don't you know that you're alive?
Carrying on solemnly as a bag of bones
Rapidly spinning through time as a passenger, rather than a
pilot of your own mind
The memory bank empties as the memories fade, and the
hours always seem to slip away
There are no more tears to cry or pain to hide
Suffering became stagnant when you finally died inside
You'll do this and do that, so what was that plan that you
hatched?
Too many wrongs to right, and the words you speak are
promising lies
However, no one buys the hype
You may change the way people see you with that smile on
your face, but only if you can cover your death filled eyes with
some night dark shades
Oh cheer up and get up, if you still can
Your dreams are documented, but run longer than your
lifespan
Your infatuation with the end wastes each day
You burn your energy with your pessimism and sad
thoughts
You're a stranger to yourself and everyone else
With every heartbeat, you see the body start to rot
Grey hairs, too many to count
You're the new meaning of down and out

You missed the moments to be brave, and your outlook
sucks
Until you change and can deal with change, well, I guess
you'll be out of luck

Isn't life fragile?

All we can do is grow and change

Some of the dead may lay awake in their eternal graves

Every smile mustn't be taken for granted

When one is floating, another is planted

Dismal outlook compounded with a flood of bad news

Believe a man when he sings the blues

For now, "They" are in the Shadows

I'm not concerned with who the C.I.A. kills at night
As long as the N.S.A. doesn't publish what I search online
Who cares about subversion for American security?
America is the brave killing machine
Peace through force and no remorse
Only dominance all the time
No recourse if the money's right
What's done in the shadows will never be brought to the
light
Truth varies with perspective and the world is connected
Too many threats to combat, The People need protected
What The People don't know, won't hurt them
Secrets are best kept till death or death comes quick
Never mind them, they're conspiracy theorists

Don't be such a Loser

All you do is bitch
In between moans
When you're watching the world fly by at warp speed
You can't find time to live a life of your own
Hypnotized by media while waiting for a glitch in the
matrix
No friends in your feed
Nobody likes your posts
You're alone in this world
A spectator
A ghost

Mission Impossible

I'm on a mission
To undo the conditioning
To revitalize the minds to tune into truth instead of sharing and liking lies
However, nobody is listening
Not to my surprise, but the circle grows smaller
Truth seekers go covert and are turned into truth keepers
As they're worried about losing their 9 to 5
But the SS of society will find them all eventually
Christians are the next victims of ruthless bigotry
Extortion, blackmail, defamation, then violence are tools of the woke brigade
Anyway, I aim to turn these hypocrites of kids into God fearing humans
Now that God's wrath is upon us, fear of society's wrath haunts us
Even if I'm persecuted, I won't change my ways
Their heads will explode when they hear what I have to say
They may hang my neck and break my bones
But they'll never be able to take my soul
I'm in it for the long game, however long it takes
I believe in redemption, truth, forgiveness, and change
Change because of truth
Change in seek of redemption
Forgiving yourself and everybody else
I hope to see more Christians rather than victims

Happy Melody

How much must this trembling and weak body suffer?
"I was promised a war, dammit", I say in a long distraught
mumble

"Well, there's something worth fighting for", I
subconsciously reassure myself
Long breathes and a racing mind
I don't fear death and I only waste time
I'm a million thoughts, thousand bottles, and a hundred
adventures packed into one crooked and sad bag of bones
Oh, this soul swirls around anxiously to become somebody
righteous before I see that final holy light
The soul refuses to sleep at night, as it casts dreams yet to
be materialized
I scream silently, as the world falls around me
This burdensome ole body has buckled and will be rebuilt as
someone beautiful.
Well, at least I'm always hopeful

LETTER FROM A FRIEND

Oh, twisted fool,
How you lust for pleasure amid depravity
Using the broken rod to smash rocks at rock bottom
Battling to fulfill your increasing wants by selling pieces of
your shattered soul
Smothering your conscious and quieting the internal
dialogue in pursuit of entertainment
Distractions buried reality in an unmarked grave
Torturous insanity only greets the sober mind
Passing
Always passing
Passing away, maniacally
Afraid to be afraid
Forgetting to feel, dumbly and willfully
So the body jumps head first into a pool of madness in
search of something divine
Cool off kid and repent
Until you seek, you'll never find
The lake of fire grows wider with each maddening moment
Your mouth mumbles nonsense and your wicked heart
commands a break
You ignore warning signs in your shapeless world
Only seeing blurred lines and unrealized remorse
Blind in time and chained by pride
Poor in confidence but rich in pain
You'll suffer in multitudes until you seek peace again
So, until then, enjoy your plague

I wish you all the best.

Your Friend,

Death

P.S. The devil has a job for you shoveling broken glass at Fiery Lake Beach. Don't be late!

(So much space, what a waste!)
You're almost done, congrats! ;)

The Left and Right Fight all the Time

Oh, cruel leftist
How you express your righteous liberalism through bigotry,
violence, cursing, arson, and intolerance
How you seek out to destroy whoever challenges you
How your evolving and perverted virtues will one day single
you out
Oh, scared conservative
Your representative forwards your emails to their junk
folder
As your patience thins, rednecks storm the center of
democracy
The very place that makes this country great, attacked by
citizens aka Right Supremacists
Don't you know all white men are racists and privileged?
Are there any consequences for broad generalizations?
You once fought against sensationalism
Now, you're hiding in the closet from the genderless
soldiers of Armageddon

Pop Culture & The News Cycle

Israel may attack Iran

And Joe Biden may be a Muppet of a man

However, nothing matters now that truth is on the lam

At least, that's what the report was

China creates it's red lines with the blood of camp workers

Well, they better be working on my iPhone!

Racist

Homophobe

Bigot

People say "I don't care", while rocking their slave-made
kicks

Pandemics are now a good way to control people

"I can't wait for this Stimulus package to hit"

Another stimulus check for the working man, who pawned his
wedding ring six months ago to make a car payment for a car
that eventually got repossessed

(He still gets taxes taken out of his part-time check)

(His part-time job is about to be lost, he can pack his things in
a Walmart sack or amazon box)

Laws kept the landlord from using his boot

While his renters eat ramen, he watches funny videos on
YouTube

There are no individuals

Just groups of racists and progress

Everybody is gay

But nobody is happy

You know the acronym

All-inclusive

Exclusivity means firing squad

Say it

Live it

Or burn

Burn any way

Literature will be shook from the shelves

Sifting out the evil and hate

Perpetual evil espouses hate

Anyway, subscribe to my link, watch me do porn on
livestream

Words will continue to evolve or devolve in meanings

The tower of babel is teetering by winds blown from right and
left directions

Valid opinions are based on a few perceptions that are called
collective

History rewritten for a better future

Corporations get bailed out instead of neutered

Future

Now

When

Then

How

What

Is

Isn't

Never why

What's the question?

Never-mind

Model your thoughts to our growing standards

Or be abandoned

Take your time

"Willful cost"

Big benefits and no freedoms back

"Give up all you have and pick up your cross"

Implant the collective desire

Sell the soul for mind control

Scroll to skip over a world on fire

Life was Simple

Life was simple when I didn't see money in a man
Now, life is dismal because I have the knowledge about
man's love affair with money
Woe, oh, money runs the land

I smile and do what I can
It's hard to dream having seen all these material things
Shimmering and blinking while begging to be idolized and
owned!

I can only wish upon stars and satellites in seek of a helping
hand

Work and time
Truth and lies
It's time to read between the lines

Salvation can only come from Christ
Until you seek, you will never find
America, the land where the lost lead the blind, open your
eyes!

While you're waiting on your bailout and restoration, I'm
praying and waiting on the wise to awaken

We need a miracle to bring humanity back to this desperate
population

Morality and charity in the form of demonstration
Awaken!

Love without a price tag
Empathy for the fellow man
More than love from these current fellow flesh bags!
More faith, commitment, accountability, compassion, and
charity in this grand awakening!

The End